THE
CHILES&PEPPERS
COOKBOOK

BASIC INGREDIENTS

— THE —
CHILES&PEPPERS
COOKBOOK

MORE THAN SIXTY
EASY, IMAGINATIVE RECIPES

EDITED BY
NICOLA HILL

COURAGE
BOOKS

AN IMPRINT OF
RUNNING PRESS BOOK PUBLISHERS

Philadelphia · London

Canadian representatives:
General Publishing Co., Ltd.,
30 Lesmill Road, Don Mills, Ontario, M3B 2T6

10 9 8 7 6 5 4 3 2 1
Digit on the right indicates the number of this printing.
Library of Congress Cataloging-in-Publication number 94-73875
ISBN 1-56138-496-8
Printed in Singapore

Acknowledgements
Executive Art Editor: Penny Stock
Designer: Louise Leffler
Commissioning Editor: Nicola Hill
Editorial Assistant: Kathy Steer
U.S. Consultant: Liz Granirer
Production Controller: Melanie Frantz
Photographer: Jeremy Hopley
Home Economist: Annie Nichols
Illustrator: Roger Gorringe/Garden Studio
Varieties text written by Jackie Gear

This edition published in the United States of America in 1995
by Courage Books, an imprint of
Running Press Book Publishers
125 South Twenty-Second Street
Philadelphia, Pennsylvania 19103-4399

Notes
Microwave methods are based on microwave ovens with a High
Power output of 800 watts.
All the jellies, jams and preserves should be processed in a boiling
water-bath canner according to the USDA guidelines.

CONTENTS

The heat and flavor of all fresh, dried and ground chiles vary, so add
small amounts first, then taste and adjust the amounts as required.
Preparing Fresh Chiles: For a hot result, break off stalk and wash the
chili under cold running water. For a milder flavor, remove the seeds
by cutting the chili in half lengthwise. Scrape out the seeds with the
point of a knife and cut away the fleshy white "ribs" from each half.
WARNING: Always take care when using chiles. After preparation,
wash your hands, knives and chopping board thoroughly and never
let any part of the chili go near your eyes.

Storage notes: Sweet peppers can be stored in a plastic bag in the
refrigerator for 2-3 days, and fresh chiles for 1 week. Dried chiles can
be kept in a dry place for up to 1 year.

Originating in South America, capsicums have been eaten and enjoyed for thousands of years, being more commonly known as chiles, peppers, capsicums, pimientos or poivrons, depending on where they are used. Botanically they fall into two main types, *Capsicum annuum longum* – the hot peppers or chiles – and *Capsicum annuum grossum* – the sweet peppers. They should not be confused with black pepper, *Piper nigrum*, which is a different species. We have Christopher Columbus to blame for this misnomer, since he, while looking for the black pepper plant, came across the capsicum, thought that he had found his precious black pepper, and named it "pepper." The name stuck! Cayenne pepper, however, is made from a chili, and paprika from a sweet pepper.

Peppers come in a myriad of shapes, sizes and colors, and vary enormously in how hot they are. The chemical responsible for the fiery heat is called *capsaicin*. It not only stimulates the palate, but also activates the brain into producing endorphins, which give us a feeling of well-being. Capsicums, especially fresh sweet peppers, are also very good for our health because they contain appreciable amounts of vitamins C and A.

Although both chiles and sweet peppers display a colorful range of yellows, oranges, reds and even purplish black, they all start off green in the unripe state. Many indeed are eaten while green, when they are more acidic, becoming milder and sweeter as the warmer colors develop. In the case of chiles, the redder and smaller they are, the hotter they taste.

Chiles and sweet peppers do best in hot climates, such as South America, the southern U.S. and the Far East, but they can also be grown outside in the warmer parts of Europe and even in parts of Canada, the northern U.S. and northern Europe, if raised in a greenhouse or plastic tunnel. They are easily killed by frost and so it is advisable, when growing outside in less hospitable climes, to choose fast-growing varieties that can be planted out in late spring and then harvested in early autumn.

Where chiles and peppers thrive, chefs select different types with great enthusiasm. American seed catalogs list 300 varieties of chili and over 150 types of sweet peppers. By contrast, British sellers only list around 20 chiles and 50 sweet peppers.

SWEET PEPPERS

Ace
A modern hybrid, bell-shaped pepper from the American seed company Burpee. A fast-maturing variety, ripening in 60 days in the U.S., and suited to growing in the U.K.

Ace

Aconcagua
This is an enormous, elongated pepper, measuring 2½ inches across at the shoulder and up to 11 inches in length, which gets its name from Mt. Aconcagua in Argentina. It is yellowish-green when unripe, with a sweet flavor. Good for salads and for cooking.

Ariane
Most peppers ripen to red but this variety matures to a bright orange. Developed by Dutch seed breeders, it ripens in just 70 days in North America. It has a superb flavor, ideal for stir-fries.

Big Bertha
Reputed to be the largest bell pepper ever produced: individual fruits measure 10 inches long and 4 inches at their widest and weigh up to 1 pound. Dark green when unripe, turning to rich red with prominent fissures in the flesh; ideal for stuffing, but can also be cooked or eaten raw. It is a mild, early-maturing variety, with the additional attribute of being resistant to the Tomato Mosaic Virus (*TMV*) disease.

Bull Nose
This appears to be declining in popularity, which is surprising as it is one of the quickest to reach maturity and a heavy cropper. A bell pepper which is squarish in shape, around 4 inches long and wide. Its thick flesh is sweet and mild, though the ribs are pungent. Also known as Sweet Bull Nose, Large Bell or Sweet Mountain.

California Wonder
Though it has been superseded by modern varieties, this Burpee selection is popular in the U.S. and is still the leading choice of commercial growers. The plants are upright and prolific, bearing numerous attractive dark green, cube-shaped fruits 4 inches across and weighing around 6 ounces. A mild-flavored, perfect stuffing pepper that freezes well.

Cherry Sweet
This is a most unusual sweet pepper, more like a small tomato or a giant cherry that has been squashed into a flattened cone. It is mostly grown by canners for pickling. The plant is a compact bush that grows less than 2 feet tall with masses of dark green fruitlets, 1 inch in diameter, ripening to deep crimson. A similar pepper, though hot, is Red Cherry.

Golden Belle

Golden Belle
This bell pepper ripens to bright yellow in under 70 days in the U.S., and it is also suitable for growing in the U.K., where it is known as Golden Belle. Its yellow color provides a good contrast to red or green peppers in salads or stir-fries.

Gypsy
A very prolific hybrid variety: over 40 medium sized, elongated cube-shaped peppers from each plant is not at all unusual. Winner of the bronze medal of the "All American Selection" and the Royal Horticultural Society's Award of Merit. Deep red when ripe and well flavored, it is also tasty in its unripe yellow-green state.

Gypsy

Italian Sweet

Italian Sweet
A pepper for the northeastern states of the U.S.; non-bell shaped, long and narrow, tapering over its 6-7 inch length from 1½-2 inches wide at the shoulder to a blunt end. It is one of the better-flavored cultivars, and has thin, sweet flesh. This pepper is also known as Long John.

Jingle Bells
If space is at a premium Jingle Bells are the peppers to grow. Each plant produces masses of bright, shiny red 1½-inch bell peppers, making this an ideal choice for container or pot growing.

Lipstick
An exceptionally early variety bearing deliciously sweet, elongated, tapering fruits, 5 inches long by 1½ inches across, which turn from dark green to a bright lipstick red color. These bell peppers grow well, even in poor sunless summers, making them suitable for most parts of North America.

Lipstick

Marconi
A massive pepper, almost 12 inches in length and 3 inches across the shoulder. The Marconi was bred by Italians and has a mild sweet flavor; it is used fresh in pizzas and salads. This pepper is often called Long Red Marconi.

Pimiento
A distinctive, scarlet, heart-shaped pepper; the pepper of Spain, and also of Hungary. Each pimiento plant bears numerous fruits which are richly aromatic and sweet at maturity. Though fresh pimientos are often used in salads, they are more commonly dried and powdered to make paprika, and in the southern U.S. they are widely cultivated for the canning industry. This variety has spawned numerous variations including Pimiento Choco with chocolate-brown fruits, Yellow Cheese with orange fruits, and Perfection, having smaller fruits which are particularly suitable for the canners.

Purple Beauty

Purple Beauty
Purple Beauty is a recent and popular development from the hybrid Purple Belle. It turns from green to a dark purple, almost black. Fruits are block shaped and thick walled, with a relatively bland, sweetish flavor.

Red Skin
This is another dwarf variety, growing only 12-18 inches tall and suitable for pots, patios and windowsills. This variety crops well even under adverse weather conditions. Bright green; slightly pointed fruits which ripen to a shiny red color.

Sweet Banana
The long, tapered shape of this sweet pepper is more akin to a hot or chili pepper; the hot equivalent is Hungarian Wax (*see page 10*). A green fruit turning to yellow/orange then red, with sweet, waxy flesh, similar in flavor to Pimiento and almost as versatile.

World Beater
Named on account of its prolific cropping: upward of 30 heavy, block-shaped fruits per plant is not uncommon. It matures in around 70 days in the U.S. and is best grown under permanent protection in the U.K.

Yolo Wonder
This pepper is one of the more common bell peppers grown in the U.S., being an improved strain of California Wonder. It produces 3½-inch wide by 4-inch long, dark green fruits with a mild flavor. The plant is compact with dense foliage that protects the fruit when the sun shines fiercely. It is gradually being superseded by the newer Yolo Wonder types that give resistance to the Tomato Mosaic Virus (*TMV*) and longer picking periods.

HOT PEPPERS
Anaheim
A bushy plant that produces masses of mild-flavored, dark green chiles turning to bright red and of medium heat, mainly for the Californian canning industry. When roasted, peeled and dried, the Anaheim becomes a Pasado, which is used to flavor soups and stews.

Apache
This is a patio variety growing no more than 18 inches tall. This extremely prolific plant produces medium-hot fruits.

Bird's Eye
This pepper is also known as Mexican Peanuts. They are tiny

bead-like peppers which are just ¼ inch across, and are said to be so hot that the juice will blister your fingers. Bird's Eye peppers are usually found growing wild in Texas and the south west U.S. They are rarely cultivated – only one U.S. seller stocks these seeds.

Cayenne
Perhaps the best-known chili pepper, although usually bought as cayenne pepper powder, which is made by crushing the dried red pods. Cayenne peppers can be grown in the U.K., where they produce long, narrow, curved pods, each 5 inches long by ¾ inch wide at the shoulder, with thin walls and a

Cayenne

bitingly hot flavor. In the U.S. they are also known as Ginnie peppers and are available in a number of varieties – Cayenne Early, Cayenne Long Slim, Cayenne Large Red Thick and Cayenne Ultra, to name a few.

Chilaca
This is a relatively mild Mexican variety with 9-inch long, twisted and flattened pods, which ripen to dark brown, hence its name which means "little raisin" in Spanish. Chilaca is rarely eaten fresh but commonly used in its dried form, when it is known as Pasilla. Dried Pasilla is essential in the preparation of Mexican *mole* and *adobados* sauces.

Chili
A small-fruited variety of pepper, produced on erect bushy plants, each around 2 inches long by ½ inch wide, tapering to a point; pale yellow-green in color when unripe, maturing to a bright red, and extremely hot in taste. This pepper is sometimes called Finger Cayenne in the U.S.

Fresno
This pepper is another Mexican cultivar of similar length to the Chili but much broader at the shoulder – 1¼ inches – gently

Chili

tapering to a rounded point, like a stump-rooted carrot. It is thick-fleshed, sweet and very hot. Used in salads and sauces but also pickled.

Habanero
This is the hottest chili of all, guaranteed to take your breath away. Although the Habanero is mainly grown in the Yucatan peninsula of Mexico and the Caribbean, its name indicates that it derives from the Cuban capital, Havana. Botanically it is *Capsicum chinense,* an entirely different species from other hot peppers, having a heart-shaped fruit just 2 inches long and 1¼ inches at its widest, narrowing to a point which, unusually for a hot pepper, ripens to a

rich golden orange color, with a fruity aroma. This chili is a slow-maturer, requiring humid tropical growing conditions.

Hungarian Wax

Hungarian Wax

The best chili pepper for growing in cool areas and therefore ideal for the U.K. and North America, where it grows easily. Hungarian Wax is the hot equivalent of the Sweet Banana pepper (*see page 8*) and it can be eaten at any stage, from unripe, when it has shiny yellow fruit, through to orange, then red, getting hotter as it ripens but staying sweet in flavor throughout. In the U.S. it is occasionally called Hot Banana or Bulgarian.

Jalapeño

America's best-known and most versatile chili. Both unripe (when green in color), and ripe (when red in color), Jalapeños are used as a topping on pizzas, an ingredient in sauces, roasted in the oven, or stuffed with meat. When dried and smoked over a wood fire, they are known as Chipotles. This is one of the earliest of the hot chili varieties, maturing in just 65 days in North America. The plant gets its name from the town of Xalapa in Veracruz, Mexico. Jalapeño produces a thick-fleshed, almost sausage-shaped fruit, 2½-3 inches long, that is blisteringly hot.

Jalapeño

Jamaican Scotch Bonnet

This pepper is closely related to the Habanero and is almost as hot, though with slightly smaller fruits. It is a Caribbean variety grown in Jamaica, where it is used in curries as well as a condiment.

Korean

This Asian variety, while originating in Korea, is widely grown in Japan and the south-western U.S. It is a fast-maturing variety and a heavy cropper, producing 4-inch long twisted pods with thin flesh, which are pale green when unripe. Available in the U.S. from specialty Asian vegetable stores.

New Mexico

Similar to an Anaheim but hotter, with 9-inch long fruits that are both straight, yet distorted. Usually picked when half-grown and still green for stuffing with meat or cheese. Resistant to the Tomato Mosaic Virus (*TMV*).

Nu Mex Sunrise

Nu Mex Sunrise is a chili pepper that ripens to a bright golden yellow when mature. It is about 6 inches long, slightly tapered and flattish, with a mild flavor. This pepper is used for its decorative qualities in Mexican rice dishes.

Peter Pepper
Not for the prudish, this grotesque chili is grown as often as not to shock rather than to eat! Nonetheless it has an excellent, penetratingly hot taste, if you can manage to forget about its appearance.

Peter Pepper

Poblano
A heart-shaped, dark green, medium-hot chili from the Puebla region of Mexico. Poblanos are never eaten raw, are always cooked, and frequently peeled and stuffed. Dried Poblanos are dark reddish brown and are called Anchos. They are the main constituent of Mexican *mole* sauces and perhaps the sweetest of the dried chiles. Poblanos are frequently confused with the longer and thinner Pasilla (*see Chilaca, page 9*). They are often available in shops in powdered form.

Rocoto
This is a perennial chili, *Capsicum pubescens,* which grows as a short-lived, small, shrubby tree of 10 feet in the high Andes, though 4 feet is more usual. At just 1 inch long and 1½ inches across at the shoulder, the Rocoto resembles a small, pointed turnip with an intensely hot fruity flavor. The Mexicans call it a *rocotillo* and use it pickled.

Serrano
The name Serrano means "from the high land" and it is grown in Mexico at quite high altitudes, where conditions are cool and moist. Serrano plants are tall, growing to almost 3 feet, and produce dozens of glossy green, 2-inch long, candle-shaped chiles, ripening to scarlet. Extremely hot when red and also sweeter than when green and unripe. Dried Serranos are known in Mexico as *serrano seco*, or *chile seco,* and are used powdered or in sauces.

Tabasco
This is another species of chili, *Capsicum frutescens*, producing tiny, 1-inch long, pencil-thin, ¼-½-inch wide fruits, on a low, bushy shrub. Used almost exclusively in the production of Tabasco sauce.

Yatsufusa
Japan's most popular hot pepper. Grown widely for the spice trade. Devilishly hot, 3-inch long, tapered green peppers, rather like Tabascos in shape, ripening to deep red. The seeds are beginning to become available in the U.S.

Yatsufusa

CHINESE CABBAGE & PEPPER SOUP

Serves 4-6

2 tablespoons corn oil
½ stick butter
½ pound sweet green peppers, cored, seeded and chopped
2 onions, chopped
½ head of Chinese cabbage, shredded
4 tablespoons all-purpose flour
1¾ cups chicken stock
1¾ cups milk
3 tablespoons light cream
salt and freshly ground black pepper

Heat the oil in a saucepan, then add the butter. Add the peppers, onions and Chinese cabbage and cook gently for 5 minutes.

Blend in the flour and cook for 1 minute. Stir in the stock and bring to a boil. Add salt and pepper to taste and simmer, covered, for 30 minutes or until the vegetables are tender.

Purée the soup in a blender or food processor, or rub through a strainer. Return to the cleaned saucepan, stir in the milk and heat through. Adjust the seasoning to taste and swirl in the cream just before serving.

RED PEPPER SOUP

Serves 4-6

1 tablespoon corn oil
1 large onion, chopped
2 garlic cloves, finely chopped
2 tablespoons dry sherry
3-4 sweet red peppers, cored, seeded and chopped
1 potato, peeled and diced
2 tablespoons tomato paste
2 large tomatoes, peeled and sliced
3½ cups hot beef stock
1 bouquet garni
salt and freshly ground black pepper

FOR GARNISH:
2-3 tablespoons plain yogurt
cracked black peppercorns
sprigs of fresh chervil

Heat the oil in a saucepan and cook the onion for 4-5 minutes. Stir in the garlic, sherry, peppers, potato, tomato paste, tomatoes and stock. Add the bouquet garni and seasoning. Stir. Bring to a boil, cover, and simmer for 30 minutes. Discard the bouquet garni and purée the soup in a blender or food processor, or rub through a strainer. Return to the cleaned saucepan, and adjust the seasoning to taste. Heat gently. Garnish with yogurt, peppercorns and chervil. Serve hot.

Illustrated opposite

SPANISH SOUP

Serves 4-6

½ cucumber, chopped
1 pound tomatoes, peeled and chopped
1 sweet red pepper, cored, seeded and chopped
1 sweet green pepper, cored, seeded
and chopped
2 large Spanish onions, chopped
1 garlic clove, chopped
½ cup fresh white bread crumbs
about 1½ cups water
2 tablespoons red wine vinegar
1 teaspoon salt
2 teaspoons olive oil
½ teaspoon paprika
chopped fresh parsley, for garnish

In a large bowl mix the cucumber, tomatoes, red and green peppers and onions with the garlic, bread crumbs, water, vinegar and salt. Work the mixture in a blender or food processor until smooth, then return it to the bowl and stir in the oil and paprika.

Cover the soup and refrigerate for 2 hours. Before serving, stir well, then ladle into chilled soup bowls and garnish with the chopped fresh parsley.

RED PEPPER & GINGER SOUP

Serves 4-6

1 stick butter
4 sweet large red peppers, cored, seeded and
coarsely chopped
2 large leeks (*mostly white part only*),
coarsely chopped
2 teaspoons ground ginger
3 teaspoons paprika
1 tablespoon sugar
shredded rind and juice of 1 large orange
2 cups chicken stock
salt and freshly ground white pepper
2 cups buttermilk or plain yogurt
FOR GARNISH:
4 tablespoons almond flakes
a little oil and butter, for cooking

Melt the butter in a large saucepan without browning. Add the peppers and leeks, cover and cook over a low heat to soften, stirring occasionally. Add the ginger, paprika, sugar, orange rind and juice, stock and 1 teaspoon each of salt and white pepper. Simmer for 30 minutes. Let cool, then purée the soup in a blender or food processor, or rub through a strainer. Chill in the refrigerator.

Stir in the buttermilk or yogurt. Chill again. Just before serving, lightly cook the almonds in oil and butter and sprinkle over the soup.

ITALIAN PEPPER SALAD

Serves 4-6

1 pound mixed colored sweet peppers, such as
red, yellow, black and white, cored, seeded
and sliced
8 small black olives, pitted
1 onion, sliced
2 teaspoons chopped fresh mixed herbs
1 teaspoon tomato paste
3 tablespoons olive oil
2 tablespoons red wine vinegar
salt and freshly ground black pepper

Put the peppers in a saucepan with the olives,
onion, herbs, tomato paste, oil, vinegar and
salt and pepper to taste. Mix well, cover with
a tight-fitting lid and bring to a boil.

Reduce the heat and simmer, covered, for 15-
20 minutes or until the peppers are just soft.
Remove from the heat and let cool.

Chill thoroughly. Adjust the seasoning to taste
and mix well just before serving.

MICROWAVE METHOD: Place the peppers,
olives, onion, herbs, tomato paste, oil, vinegar
and seasoning in a casserole dish. Cook on
High for 8-9 minutes, stirring twice. Chill.

Illustrated on cover

MEXICAN SALAD

Serves 8

6 ounces dried butter beans, or
1 can (*about 14 ounces*) butter beans, drained
1 sweet green pepper, cored, seeded
and chopped
1 sweet red pepper, cored, seeded and chopped
1 fresh hot chili, finely chopped
4 tomatoes, chopped
2 onions, chopped
2 garlic cloves, crushed
2 tablespoons chopped fresh parsley

DRESSING:
2 tablespoons olive oil
1 tablespoon wine vinegar
1 tablespoon lemon juice
1 teaspoon brown sugar
dash of Tabasco sauce
salt and freshly ground black pepper

If using dried beans, soak them in cold water
overnight or for at least 6-8 hours. Drain and
place them in a large saucepan with plenty of
fresh water and bring to a boil. Cover and
reduce the heat. Simmer for 1½-2 hours.
Drain well and let cool.

Place all of the salad ingredients in a bowl and
mix. To make the dressing, put all of the
dressing ingredients in a screw-top jar and
shake well. Pour over the salad, toss well and
leave in the refrigerator to marinate for at
least 1 hour before serving.

TABBOULEH WITH PEPPERS

Serves 6

1 pound burghul or cracked wheat
1 sweet green pepper, cored, seeded and
finely chopped
1 sweet red pepper, cored, seeded and
finely chopped
6 ounces button mushrooms, sliced
1½ tablespoons corn oil
1 bunch of scallions, thinly sliced
½ cup French dressing
1 tablespoon chopped fresh mint or parsley

Put the burghul or cracked wheat into a bowl and cover with cold water. Let stand for at least 2 hours or overnight. Drain the burghul or cracked wheat thoroughly, spread out on paper towels and let dry.

Put the chopped peppers in a saucepan of cold water, bring to a boil and boil for about 1 minute. Drain, rinse under cold water and drain again thoroughly.

Sauté the mushrooms gently in the oil for about 2-3 minutes. Mix with the peppers and scallions and then add the French dressing and chopped fresh mint or parsley. Add the burghul or cracked wheat and toss the mixture evenly. Turn into a large salad bowl, cover with plastic wrap and chill until required.

CHICKPEA & RED PEPPER SALAD

Serves 4

6 ounces dried chickpeas, soaked overnight
and drained
3 sweet red peppers
12 black olives, pitted
2 tablespoons chopped fresh cilantro
thin strips of orange rind, for garnish
DRESSING:
3 tablespoons corn oil
½ teaspoon shredded orange rind
2 tablespoons orange juice
1 garlic clove, crushed
salt and freshly ground black pepper

Cook the chickpeas in unsalted boiling water for 2 hours, or until they are tender. Cook the red peppers under a hot broiler for 15 minutes, turning them frequently, until the skins blacken and blister. Hold the peppers under cold water and, using a small, sharp knife, peel off the skins. Halve the peppers, remove the cores and seeds and slice them.

Mix the dressing ingredients together. Drain the chickpeas and toss in the dressing while they are still hot. Set aside to cool. Stir in the peppers and olives and half of the cilantro. Turn the salad into a serving dish and sprinkle over the remaining cilantro and orange rind.

Illustrated opposite

PROVENCAL PEPPER SALAD

Serves 6

2 large sweet green peppers
2 large sweet red peppers
8 tablespoons olive oil
3 tablespoons tarragon vinegar
2 garlic cloves, finely chopped
2 tablespoons finely chopped fresh mixed herbs,
such as parsley, thyme and chervil
6 tomatoes, peeled and thickly sliced
6 hard-boiled eggs, thickly sliced
24 anchovy fillets
24 black olives, pitted
salt and freshly ground black pepper

Cook the peppers under a hot broiler, turning frequently, until the skins blacken and blister. Peel off the skins under cold running water. Halve the peppers, then remove the cores and seeds and cut each half lengthwise into 3 or 4 strips. Pat dry with paper towels.

Prepare the dressing by combining the oil, vinegar, garlic and seasoning, but do not add too much salt as the anchovy fillets are very salty. Stir in the herbs.

Layer the peppers, tomatoes and eggs in a bowl, sprinkling each layer with dressing. Arrange the anchovy fillets and olives in a lattice on the top. Leave in the refrigerator to marinate for 30 minutes before serving chilled.

MIXED PEPPERS WITH TUNA & CAPERS

Serves 6

6 large mixed colored sweet peppers
4 tablespoons olive oil
1 teaspoon lemon juice
1 garlic clove, crushed
1 can (*about 7 ounces*) tuna, drained and flaked
1 tablespoon capers
salt and freshly ground black pepper
sprigs of fresh parsley, for garnish

Cook the peppers under a hot broiler for about 15 minutes, turning from time to time, until the skins are blackened and blistered all over. Peel off the skins under cold running water, then cut each pepper lengthwise into 3 strips, discarding the cores and seeds. Rinse under cold water to remove all traces of skin and seeds, then pat dry with paper towels.

Put the pepper strips in a bowl with the oil, lemon juice, garlic and a little salt and pepper. Let marinate for 30 minutes, stirring occasionally. Drain, reserving the marinade. Lay the pepper strips flat.

Mix the tuna and capers together. Put a generous spoonful on each pepper strip and roll up. Arrange the rolls in a shallow serving dish with the colors alternating. Pour the marinade over, garnish with parsley and serve.

CHICKEN & PEPPER PASTA SALAD WITH ROQUEFORT DRESSING

Serves 4-6

1 tablespoon extra virgin olive oil
½ pound small dried pasta shapes
½ pound cooked chicken, chopped
1 sweet red pepper, cored, seeded and finely chopped
1 sweet yellow or sweet orange pepper, cored, seeded and finely chopped
1-2 tablespoons chopped fresh herbs, such as parsley and thyme
salt and freshly ground black pepper
a few black olives, pitted, for garnish

DRESSING:
2 ounces Roquefort, Gorgonzola, or blue Brie cheese
2 tablespoons extra virgin olive oil
2 tablespoons mayonnaise
2 teaspoons white wine vinegar
1 garlic clove, crushed

Bring a large saucepan of water to a boil, swirl in the oil and add a large pinch of salt. Add the pasta and boil, uncovered, over a moderate heat for 10 minutes, or according to the package directions, until al dente.

Meanwhile, make the dressing. Put the cheese in a large bowl and mash with a fork. Add the remaining dressing ingredients and stir vigorously until thick and evenly blended.

Drain the pasta thoroughly, then turn into the bowl of dressing and toss well to coat. Add salt and pepper to taste, toss again until all the ingredients are evenly combined, then let the salad cool to room temperature.

Add the cooked chicken, peppers and herbs to the salad and toss well until all the ingredients are evenly combined. Transfer to a large serving bowl and garnish with the olives. Serve the pasta salad at room temperature.

BEAN SPROUT & RED PEPPER SALAD

Serves 4
12 ounces bean sprouts
1 sweet red pepper, cored, seeded and chopped
1 small onion, sliced
1 large carrot, coarsely shredded
DRESSING:
1 teaspoon sugar
2 teaspoons Dijon mustard
1 tablespoon wine vinegar
1 tablespoon soy sauce
2 tablespoons olive oil
salt and freshly ground black pepper

Put the bean sprouts, red pepper, onion and carrot in a large serving bowl.

To make the dressing, put the sugar, mustard, vinegar and soy sauce in a small bowl and whisk together, then gradually beat in the oil. Season with salt and pepper. Pour the dressing over the vegetables and toss the salad well before serving.

OKRA WITH CHILES

Serves 4
3 tablespoons butter
1 large onion, sliced
3 garlic cloves, sliced
1-inch piece of fresh ginger, peeled and finely chopped or shredded
2 fresh red chiles, finely chopped
½ teaspoon chili powder
1 pound okra, topped and tailed
1 cup water
2 teaspoons unsweetened dehydrated coconut
salt

Melt the butter in a heavy saucepan, then add the onion, garlic, ginger, chiles and chili powder. Sauté gently for 5 minutes, until soft, stirring occasionally.

Add the okra, the measured water and salt to taste. Bring to a boil, then lower the heat, cover and simmer for 5-10 minutes, until the okra are just tender, but still firm to the bite. Sprinkle with the coconut and serve hot.

Illustrated opposite

TURKISH STUFFED PEPPERS

Serves 6

1 cup short-grain rice
6 large sweet green peppers
8 tablespoons olive oil
2 large mild onions, finely chopped
⅓ cup currants
2 tablespoons pine nuts
1 teaspoon sugar
6 tablespoons finely chopped fresh parsley
salt and freshly ground black pepper

Put the rice in a strainer and rinse it thoroughly under cold running water. Pour a tea kettleful of boiling water over the rice and leave it to drain in the strainer for 1 hour.

Carefully cut the top off each pepper and reserve the tops for later. Scrape out the seeds and pith, taking care not to pierce the skins. Rinse the peppers under cold running water to remove any remaining seeds and leave the peppers to drain, upside down, while the filling is being prepared.

Heat the oil in a large skillet. Add the onions and cook, stirring, until translucent and light golden in color. Stir in the rice, currants and pine nuts. Season to taste with the sugar, salt and pepper. Continue to cook over a moderate heat, stirring constantly, until the rice is golden. Stir in the chopped parsley.

Fill the peppers with the rice mixture, leaving a small space at the top for the rice to expand. Cover with the reserved pepper tops.

Put the upright peppers close together in a heavy saucepan just large enough to take them in one layer. Carefully pour in enough boiling water to come halfway up the sides of the peppers. Place the saucepan over the heat and bring the water back to simmering point. Cover, reduce the heat and cook the peppers very gently for 45-60 minutes, or until the rice is tender. If necessary, add more boiling water as the peppers are cooking. Let the peppers cool in the saucepan before removing them to a serving dish. Serve chilled.

ZUCCHINI WITH PEPPERS

Serves 4

4 zucchini, halved lengthwise
5 tablespoons olive oil
1 teaspoon salt
4 tomatoes, peeled, seeded and chopped
1 garlic clove, crushed
3 sprigs of fresh basil, chopped
2 sweet yellow peppers, cored, seeded and cut
into strips
6 ounces Gruyère cheese, thinly sliced
4 anchovy fillets, halved lengthwise

Blanch the zucchini for 2 minutes in salted boiling water and drain thoroughly. Grease an ovenproof dish with a little of the oil, put the zucchini in the dish and sprinkle them with ½ teaspoon of the salt. Cook until the skins brown and split, then remove the skins. Put the skinless zucchini back in the dish.

Heat 2 tablespoons of the oil in a large skillet, add the tomatoes, garlic, three-quarters of the basil and the remaining salt, and simmer for 20 minutes over a low heat.

Spread the tomato mixture and pepper strips over the zucchini and cover with the cheese slices. Top with the anchovy fillets and sprinkle with the remaining oil and basil. Brown in a preheated oven, 425°F, for about 15 minutes, then serve immediately.

HARICOT BEANS IN PEPPER CREAM SAUCE

Serves 4

1 can (*about 14 ounces*) haricot beans
1 sweet red pepper, cored, seeded and cut
into strips
1 teaspoon paprika
pinch of chili powder
1 tablespoon butter
2 teaspoons all-purpose flour
½ cup heavy cream
2 tablespoons fresh or bottled
green peppercorns
1 tablespoon chopped fresh parsley
salt and cayenne pepper

Put the canned beans with their juice in a large saucepan. Add the strips of pepper, paprika and chili powder. Bring slowly to a boil, then reduce the heat.

Meanwhile, melt the butter in another saucepan. Add the flour and cook for about 1 minute. Add a little of the bean liquid and the cream a little at a time, mixing well after each addition. Add the peppercorns and parsley and cook over a gentle heat for 2-3 minutes.

Pour the pepper sauce over the beans, season with salt and cayenne pepper to taste, and mix well. Bring to a boil, stirring constantly. Serve hot. This dish is ideal with sausages.

EGGPLANT & CHILI KABOBS

Makes 4-6 kabobs

1 pound eggplants, cut into 1-inch pieces
9 tablespoons olive oil
2 sweet yellow peppers, seeded and cut into
1-inch squares
2-3 fresh green chiles, seeded and cut into
fine rings
salt and freshly ground black pepper

Place the pieces of eggplant in one layer on a large flat plate, then sprinkle heavily with salt and let them stand for 30 minutes – this draws out the juices which may make the eggplants taste bitter. Rinse the eggplant pieces thoroughly under cold running water, then pat dry with paper towels.

Arrange the eggplant on the plate again and brush with half the oil, coating each piece on all sides. Leave for 15 minutes.

Thread the eggplant onto metal or soaked bamboo skewers, alternating with squares of pepper, and adding a ring of chili every 2-3 pieces. Cook on the oiled grill of a preheated barbecue for 5 minutes, then baste with the remaining oil and turn and cook for a further 10 minutes, until crisp. Serve the kabobs as an accompaniment to meat or fish dishes.

Illustrated on page 1

THREE-PEPPER KABOBS

Makes 8 kabobs

6 mixed colored sweet peppers, such as red,
orange and white, cored, seeded and cut into
1½-inch squares
about ½ cup olive oil
2 garlic cloves, finely chopped
salt
1 tablespoon crushed black peppercorns
3 tablespoons lemon juice

Thread the peppers onto 8 metal or soaked bamboo skewers, alternating the colors. A medium pepper will normally make about 12-16 pieces so there should be about 3-4 pieces of each pepper color on each skewer.

Brush the peppers generously on all sides with the oil and cook under a preheated broiler for about 7-10 minutes, turning and basting with oil every 1-2 minutes. When the peppers are just beginning to blacken they are done. Baste again with olive oil.

Put the skewers on serving plates, then sprinkle each one with a little of the finely chopped garlic, generously season with salt and pepper and then pour over the lemon juice. Serve immediately.

Illustrated opposite

SAUTEED PEPPERS WITH TOMATOES & BACON

Serves 4

2 tablespoons corn oil
2 ounces bacon slices, chopped
1½ pounds sweet green and/or yellow peppers,
cored, seeded and cut into fairly large pieces
3 tomatoes, peeled and cut into wedges
1 garlic clove, crushed
3-4 tablespoons beef stock
1 sprig of fresh basil or dill, chopped
1-2 tablespoons sour cream
salt and freshly ground black pepper

Heat the oil in a saucepan, add the bacon and cook until crisp. Add the peppers, tomatoes and garlic and cook for about 5 minutes, stirring continuously. Add the stock, herbs and salt and pepper to taste. Simmer, over a low heat, for a further 3-4 minutes.

Add the sour cream to the pepper mixture and heat gently until it is thickened. Serve immediately as an accompaniment to broiled fish or poultry.

CAULIFLOWER & PEPPER CURRY

Serves 4

½ cup corn oil
1 tablespoon cumin seeds
1 pound cauliflower, broken into flowerets
1 large sweet green pepper, cored, seeded and
cut into strips
1 teaspoon turmeric
1-2 fresh green chiles, seeded and
finely chopped
1 garlic clove, crushed
1 cup sour cream
salt

Heat the oil in a large saucepan and sauté the cumin seeds until they crackle. Reduce the heat and add the cauliflower. Reserve 4 strips of pepper for garnishing and add the rest to the saucepan. Add the turmeric, chiles, garlic and salt to taste, and mix thoroughly.

Partly cover the saucepan and cook until the vegetables are tender and dry. Toss the mixture frequently during the cooking time.

Stir the sour cream into the vegetable mixture and heat through without boiling. Garnish with the reserved pepper strips and serve with plain boiled rice.

CHILES RELLENOS

Serves 3-6
corn oil, for deep-frying
6 large (*Poblano or New Mexico*) fresh chiles
6 ounces Cheddar cheese, cut into
6 sticks
3 eggs, separated
¼ cup all-purpose flour
TO SERVE:
a little chili sauce (*see page 63*)
2 ounces Cheddar cheese, shredded

To peel the chiles, heat the oil in a deep-fat fryer to 375°F. Add the whole chiles and fry until they blister. Remove the chiles, let cool, then carefully peel off the skins.

Cut a small slit in each chili and remove the seeds, leaving on the stems. Dry well with paper towels. Put a stick of cheese inside each chili. Beat the egg whites until stiff. Lightly beat the egg yolks and fold in the whites. Roll the chiles in the flour, then dip into the egg mixture to coat evenly.

Heat the oil in a deep-fat fryer to 350°F or until a cube of bread browns in 30 seconds. Deep fry the chiles until brown, turning occasionally. Drain on paper towels, then place in a shallow ovenproof dish and top with the chili sauce and cheese. Place under a hot broiler to melt the cheese before serving.

Illustrated on pages 2-3

PEPERONATA

Serves 8
3 tablespoons olive oil
2 tablespoons butter
1 onion, sliced
2 sweet red peppers, cored, seeded and sliced
2 sweet yellow peppers, cored, seeded and sliced
2 garlic cloves, crushed
1 pound tomatoes, peeled, quartered
and seeded
salt and freshly ground black pepper

Heat the oil and butter together in a large saucepan and gently cook the onion until softened. Add the peppers and garlic, cover and cook for 10-15 minutes over a low heat, stirring occasionally.

Add the tomatoes, and season to taste. Cover the saucepan and cook for a further 10-15 minutes, stirring occasionally. Serve hot.

MICROWAVE METHOD: Place 1 tablespoon of the oil, with the butter and onion, in a casserole dish and cook on High for 3 minutes. Add the peppers and garlic, cover and cook on High for 6-7 minutes, stirring twice. Add the tomatoes and cook on High for 5-6 minutes. Season and then serve.

CREAMED PEPPERS WITH DILL

Serves 4

½ stick butter
1 pound sweet green or red peppers, cored,
seeded and cut into thick strips
1 small onion, chopped
½ cup light cream
2 tablespoons chopped fresh dill
salt

Melt the butter in a heavy saucepan and sauté the pepper strips and chopped onion gently until soft. Season well with salt, pour in the cream and add the chopped dill. Heat through gently. Serve the creamed peppers as an accompaniment to roast pork, beef or lamb.

PEPPERS WITH BROWN RICE & WALNUT STUFFING

Serves 4

2 tablespoons corn oil
1 onion, chopped
1 large garlic clove, crushed
¼ cup brown rice
1 bay leaf
1½ cups tomato juice
1 teaspoon dried basil
2 ounces Cheddar cheese, shredded
½ cup walnuts, chopped
4 sweet red or yellow peppers, cored, seeded
and cut in half lengthwise
salt and freshly ground black pepper
shavings of Parmesan cheese, for garnish

Heat the oil in a saucepan, add the onion and garlic and cook, stirring, for 10 minutes. Add the rice, bay leaf and half the tomato juice. Cover and simmer for 40 minutes, or until the rice is tender. Discard the bay leaf. Add the basil, cheese and walnuts and season to taste.

Fill the peppers with the rice mixture and place in a greased casserole dish. Pour the remaining tomato juice around the peppers. Bake in a preheated oven, 350°F, for about 30-40 minutes. Garnish the peppers with shavings of Parmesan cheese.

Illustrated opposite

PROVENCAL BAKED TOMATOES & PEPPERS

Serves 4-6

4 Marmande tomatoes, sliced
2 sweet yellow peppers, cored, seeded and cut
into thin strips
4 tablespoons olive oil
1 garlic clove, chopped
2 tablespoons chopped fresh mixed herbs, such
as basil, thyme, rosemary and parsley, or
2 teaspoons dried mixed herbs
2 tablespoons fresh white bread crumbs
salt and freshly ground black pepper

Layer the tomatoes and peppers in a small ovenproof dish, seasoning each layer with olive oil, garlic, herbs and salt and pepper, finishing with a layer of tomatoes.

Sprinkle with the bread crumbs, then bake in a preheated oven, 425°F, for about 20-25 minutes, until the top is browned and crisp. Serve warm.

MICROWAVE METHOD: Layer the tomatoes and peppers in a 9-inch round ovenproof dish, seasoning each layer as above. Cover and cook on High for 7-8 minutes or until just tender. Sprinkle with bread crumbs and place under a preheated broiler to brown.

RED PEPPER RICE

Serves 6-8

3½ cups vegetable stock
2 cups long-grain rice
1 onion, chopped
3-4 sweet red peppers, cored, seeded
and chopped
1 tablespoon butter
1 teaspoon paprika
salt

Place the stock in a pan, bring to a boil, add the rice and a little salt. Lower the heat and cook for 20 minutes, until the rice is tender.

Meanwhile, purée the onion and red peppers in a blender or food processor until smooth. Drain the rice if necessary. Return to the saucepan and stir in the onion and pepper purée, the butter and paprika, mixing well. Adjust the seasoning to taste.

Spoon into oiled individual molds or a large ring mold and turn out onto a flat dish. Serve immediately. This is a good accompaniment to beef goulash or chicken fricassee.

MICROWAVE METHOD: Place the hot stock with the rice in a large casserole dish and cook on High for 15 minutes. Purée the onion and red pepper as above. Drain the rice if necessary. Stir in the onion and pepper purée, butter and paprika. Cook on High for 2 minutes. Finish as above.

MUSHROOM-STUFFED PEPPERS

Serves 4

4 large sweet red or sweet green peppers

oil, for brushing

4 tablespoons butter

1 onion, chopped

1 pound mushrooms, chopped

2 eggs, beaten

4 tablespoons Cheddar cheese, shredded

salt and freshly ground black pepper

Place the peppers on a baking sheet and brush lightly with the oil. Bake in a preheated oven, 400°F, for about 15-20 minutes, or until just tender. Hold the peppers with a cloth and carefully cut off the tops. Remove the cores and seeds.

Melt the butter in a saucepan and gently cook the onion until soft. Add the mushrooms and cook until the juice evaporates. Season to taste with salt and pepper, then stir in the beaten eggs. Cook until the eggs are set. Use this mixture to stuff the peppers.

Sprinkle with the shredded cheese and place under a preheated broiler for a few minutes to melt the cheese. Serve hot.

PROVENCAL RICE

Serves 4

2 tablespoons corn oil

½ pound zucchini, sliced

1 sweet red pepper, cored, seeded and chopped

1 sweet yellow pepper, cored, seeded and chopped

4 tomatoes, peeled and quartered

2 onions, sliced

a little dried marjoram

1 cup long-grain rice

2 cups vegetable stock

1 sprig of fresh thyme

1 bay leaf

2 garlic cloves, crushed

6 ounces French beans, sliced

salt and freshly ground black pepper

3 ounces Gruyère cheese, shredded, to serve (*optional*)

Heat the oil in a large saucepan. Stir in the zucchini, peppers, tomatoes and onions. Cook the mixture over a high heat for 5 minutes, stirring continuously. Season with salt, pepper and marjoram to taste. Reduce the heat and simmer for 5 minutes, stirring occasionally.

Add the rice and cook for 3 minutes before adding the stock, thyme, bay leaf and garlic. Bring to a boil and add the beans. Reduce the heat, cover and simmer for 15 minutes or until the rice and beans are tender and the liquid is absorbed. Serve with cheese, if you like.

PEPPER & TOMATO PANCAKES

Serves 4

PANCAKES:
½ cup whole wheat flour
1 large egg, beaten
1 egg yolk
½ cup milk
½ cup water
2 tablespoons melted butter or oil
extra butter or oil, for cooking

FILLING:
1½ pounds sweet red peppers
2 tablespoons olive oil
1 onion, chopped
3 pounds tomatoes, peeled, seeded
and chopped
2 tablespoons chopped fresh parsley (*optional*)
salt and freshly ground black pepper

TO FINISH:
1 cup sour cream or thick yogurt
paprika

Make the filling first. Cook the peppers under a hot broiler, turning frequently, until the skins blacken and blister. Peel off the skins under cold running water. Remove the cores and seeds and cut into small pieces.

Heat the oil in a large heavy saucepan and gently cook the onion until soft, add the peppers and tomatoes and cook, uncovered, for about 30 minutes, until the mixture is fairly thick and dry. Stir frequently towards the end of the cooking time to prevent burning. Season to taste, adding the chopped parsley, if you like.

Meanwhile, make the pancakes. Put all the ingredients and ½ teaspoon of salt into a blender or food processor and work until smooth. Alternatively, sift the flour and ½ teaspoon of salt into a bowl, mix in the eggs, then gradually add the milk, water and butter or oil to make a smooth, fairly thin batter. Heat 1 teaspoon of butter or a little oil in a small skillet; when it sizzles, pour off the excess butter or oil, so that the pan is just glistening. Keeping the skillet over a high heat, give the batter a quick stir, then put 2 tablespoons into the pan, tipping it so the batter covers the bottom of the skillet. Cook for about 30 seconds, until the top is set and the underside is tinged golden brown. Flip the pancake over and cook the other side. Remove the pancake with a spatula and put it onto a warmed plate. Make about 12 more pancakes, piling them up on top of each other, interleaved with waxed paper. Keep the pancakes warm.

To serve, put a spoonful of the filling on each pancake and roll up neatly. Spoon the cream or yogurt over the pancakes, and sprinkle with paprika. Serve at once with a salad of rocket and yellow cherry tomatoes.

Illustrated opposite

SPANISH PEPPER OMELET

Serves 4

2 tablespoons olive oil
1 onion, thinly sliced
1 sweet green pepper, cored, seeded and thinly sliced
1 large potato, boiled until just tender, and sliced
2 tomatoes, peeled, seeded and chopped
1 garlic clove, crushed
6 eggs, lightly beaten
1 tablespoon chopped fresh parsley or mixed herbs
salt and freshly ground black pepper

Heat the olive oil in a large skillet. Add the onion, pepper and potato and gently sauté for 3 minutes, or until the onion is soft and translucent. Add the tomatoes and garlic. Season to taste with salt and pepper. Cook for 2 minutes more.

Season the eggs with salt and pepper and pour over the cooked vegetables. Cook, stirring occasionally from the outside to the center. When the omelet is almost set, lower the heat and stop stirring.

When the omelet is just set and lightly brown underneath, remove the pan from the heat. Sprinkle the omelet with chopped herbs and serve immediately, cut into wedges.

SPAGHETTI WITH PEPPER SAUCE

Serves 4

about 1 pound dried spaghetti
1 tablespoon butter
SAUCE:
4 tablespoons olive oil
2 sweet red peppers, cored, seeded and cut into strips
1 can (*about 8 ounces*) tomatoes
6-8 black olives, pitted
1 anchovy fillet, finely chopped
1 sprig of fresh parsley, chopped
1 garlic clove, crushed
1 fresh green chili, seeded and cut into fine rings
1 teaspoon sugar
salt

Cook the spaghetti in salted boiling water for 12 minutes, or according to the package directions, until al dente. Drain thoroughly.

Meanwhile, make the sauce. Heat the oil in a pan, add the peppers and cook for 5 minutes. Add the tomatoes with their juice, and the olives, anchovy, parsley and garlic, mixing to break up the tomatoes. Simmer gently for 8-10 minutes. Add the chili, sugar and salt to taste.

Toss the spaghetti in the butter and place in a serving dish. Pour the sauce over the spaghetti and toss before serving.

PENNE WITH PEPPERS & ANCHOVIES

Serves 4

5 anchovy fillets
a little milk
1 sweet yellow pepper
1 sweet red pepper
1 cup vegetable stock
2 garlic cloves
½ cup corn oil
3 tablespoons dry white wine
1 tablespoon tomato paste
12 ounces dried small penne pasta
salt and freshly ground black pepper
1 tablespoon chopped fresh parsley, for garnish

Soak the anchovy fillets in a little milk to remove the excess salt.

Place the peppers on an oiled baking sheet and put in a preheated oven, 425°F, turning occasionally, until the skins are blackened and blistered. Remove from the oven and carefully peel off the skins; remove and discard the stems and seeds, collecting any pepper juices in a bowl. Using a knife and fork, cut the peppers into 1 x ¼-inch strips. Heat the stock.

Put the garlic and drained anchovy fillets through a mincer or use a food processor. Heat the oil in a large saucepan, add the anchovy and garlic mixture and cook over a low heat until softened. Add the strips of pepper, stir, and moisten with the reserved pepper juices. Season lightly, pour in the wine and allow it to evaporate slowly, then add the tomato paste diluted with the hot stock.

While the sauce is simmering, cook the pasta in a large saucepan of lightly salted boiling water for 12 minutes, or according to the package directions, until al dente. Drain thoroughly and transfer to the pan with the sauce. Mix well and pour into a deep serving dish. Garnish with chopped fresh parsley.

BAKED PASTA & PEPPERS

Serves 4

2 large sweet yellow peppers, cored, seeded and
finely chopped
½ onion, thinly sliced
6 plum tomatoes, peeled and chopped
1 cup vegetable stock
12 ounces dried penne pasta
½ teaspoon chopped fresh basil
7 ounces mozzarella cheese, diced
3 tablespoons milk
salt and freshly ground black pepper

Put the peppers in a saucepan with the onion,
tomatoes and a pinch of salt; cover and
simmer for about 20 minutes, adding the stock
after 5 minutes.

Meanwhile, cook the pasta in plenty of lightly
salted boiling water for 12 minutes, or
according to the package directions, until al
dente, then drain thoroughly.

Sprinkle the basil over the pepper sauce,
adjust the seasoning to taste, then mix with
the drained pasta and the diced mozzarella.
Transfer to a large greased ovenproof dish,
pour over the milk and place in a preheated
oven, 400°F, for about 15 minutes or until
golden brown and hot. Serve the pasta with a
mixed salad.

CHILI FETTUCCINE

Serves 4

4 tablespoons olive oil
12 ounces fresh fettuccine
2 garlic cloves, crushed
2 fresh red chiles, seeded and chopped
2 ounces button mushrooms, sliced
4 tablespoons balsamic vinegar
2 tablespoons orange juice
3 tablespoons ready-made red pesto
1 bunch of scallions, shredded
2 tablespoons toasted hazelnuts, chopped
salt

Bring plenty of water to a boil in a large
saucepan. Add a dash of oil and a pinch of
salt. Add the fettuccine and cook for about
4-6 minutes or until it rises to the surface of
the boiling water.

Meanwhile, heat the remaining oil in a large
pan. Add the garlic, chiles and mushrooms
and gently cook for 2 minutes. Reduce the
heat and stir in the remaining ingredients.

Drain the pasta well and add it to the garlic
and chili mixture, tossing well. Serve at once.

Illustrated opposite

MOZZARELLA & PEPPER PIZZA

Serves 4-6

BASE:
½ cup self-rising flour, plus extra
for dusting
½ cup whole wheat flour
1 teaspoon baking powder
½ stick margarine
½ cup milk

TOPPING:
2 tablespoons tomato chutney
2 tablespoons tomato paste
1 teaspoon Worcestershire sauce
1 tablespoon corn oil
1 large onion, finely sliced
3 large tomatoes, sliced
1 teaspoon dried mixed herbs
6 ounces mozzarella cheese, thinly sliced
½ sweet green pepper, cored, seeded and cut
into rings
½ sweet yellow pepper, cored, seeded and cut
into rings
½ sweet red pepper, cored, seeded and cut
into rings
6 stuffed olives, sliced

For the base, place the flours and baking powder into a large bowl. Add the margarine and, using your fingertips, rub in until the mixture resembles fine bread crumbs. Add the milk and mix to make a firm dough. Turn the dough out onto a lightly floured surface and knead until smooth. Roll out to a circle about 11 inches in diameter and place on an oiled baking sheet. Pinch the edge of the dough to make a rim.

For the topping, mix together the tomato chutney, tomato paste and Worcestershire sauce, then spread over the pizza base. Heat the oil in a saucepan and sauté the onion for 5 minutes. Remove with a slotted spoon and place on the pizza. Arrange the tomato slices on top and sprinkle with the herbs. Top with the cheese slices, pepper rings and sliced olives and cook in a preheated oven, 400°F, for about 20-25 minutes. Serve the pizza hot with a mixed salad.

CHAKCHOUKA

Serves 4-6

6 tablespoons olive oil
1 large onion, finely chopped
1 sweet green pepper, cored, seeded and cut
into strips
1 red pepper, cored, seeded and cut into strips
1 large garlic clove, crushed
1 pound tomatoes, coarsely chopped
6 eggs
salt and freshly ground black pepper
warm pita bread, to serve

Heat the olive oil in a shallow skillet. Sauté the onion and peppers gently for 10 minutes. Add the garlic and tomatoes and cook fairly briskly for a further 8-10 minutes, stirring.

Beat the eggs in a bowl and season with salt and pepper; add to the skillet and stir over the heat until the vegetable and egg mixture is creamy but still soft.

Serve the chakchouka immediately with pieces of warm pita bread.

MICROWAVE METHOD: Place 3 tablespoons of the oil, the onion and the peppers in a casserole dish and cook on High for 6 minutes, stirring twice. Add garlic and tomatoes. Cover and cook on High for 7-8 minutes, stirring twice. Mix eggs and seasoning together. Add and cook on High for 3 minutes or until creamy, stirring 2-3 times.

PEPPERS WITH CHICKEN RAGOUT

Serves 4

4 sweet red or green peppers
½ stick butter
1 onion, chopped
2 boneless, skinless chicken breasts, chopped
4 ounces mushrooms, sliced
½ cup light cream
pinch of freshly grated nutmeg
1 tablespoon lemon juice
salt and freshly ground black pepper

Slice the tops off the peppers and remove and discard the cores and seeds. Blanch the peppers in salted boiling water for 5 minutes, then let drain upside down.

Melt the butter in a large saucepan and gently cook the onion until soft. Add the chicken pieces and cook over a low heat for about 10-15 minutes or until cooked through and tender. Add the mushrooms and cook for a few minutes more. Pour in the cream and season to taste with salt, pepper and nutmeg. Remove from the heat and stir in the lemon juice. Use this mixture to stuff the peppers.

Place the peppers in an ovenproof dish and pour over any remaining chicken mixture. Cover and bake in a preheated oven, 350°F, for 20-25 minutes or until the peppers are tender. Serve hot with rice or creamy mashed potatoes and vegetables.

FETA & ROASTED PEPPER PIE

Serves 6

DOUGH:

¾ cup whole wheat flour

¾ cup all-purpose flour, plus extra for dusting

¾ stick butter

¾ cup water

beaten egg, to glaze

FILLING:

3 carrots, cut into thin strips

½ pound celeriac, cut into thin strips

2 parsnips, cut into thin strips

1 sweet red pepper, cored, seeded and thickly sliced

1 sweet yellow pepper, cored, seeded and thickly sliced

3 garlic cloves, halved

4 tablespoons olive oil

2 teaspoons chopped fresh rosemary

6 ounces cherry tomatoes, halved

6 ounces feta cheese, cubed

2 ounces Parmesan cheese, shredded

salt and freshly ground black pepper

To make the filling, place the carrots, celeriac, parsnips and peppers in a roasting pan. Add the garlic, oil and rosemary; season with salt and pepper. Toss the vegetables in the oil until they are coated. Bake in a preheated oven, 400°F, for 30-35 minutes, until the vegetables have started to brown and are tender.

Meanwhile, make the dough. Mix the flours and 1 teaspoon of salt in a bowl. Melt the butter with the water in a saucepan. Add to the flour and mix quickly to a soft dough. Wrap closely and let rest at room temperature for 15 minutes.

Roll out two-thirds of the dough on a lightly floured surface and use to line a greased 8-inch pie pan. Spread one-third of the vegetable mixture over the pie pan. Sprinkle one-third of the tomatoes over the top, followed by one-third of the feta and one-third of the Parmesan. Repeat twice, with the remaining ingredients.

Roll out the remaining dough to a round, large enough to cover the pie. Dampen the edges of the pie lightly with water and cover with the dough lid. Trim the edges, reserving the trimmings. Pinch the edge of the pie to seal, then make a hole in the center to allow the steam to escape.

Roll out the dough trimmings and cut into decorative leaf shapes. Attach to the pie with a little beaten egg, then brush the top of the pie all over with egg. Bake in a preheated oven, 400°F, for 40-50 minutes, until the dough is crisp and golden brown. Cool the pie in the pan for 10 minutes, then remove and serve warm.

Illustrated opposite

GOUGERE WITH RATATOUILLE

Serves 4

½ stick butter or margarine
½ cup water
6 tablespoons whole wheat flour
2 eggs, beaten
½ teaspoon English mustard
2 ounces Cheddar cheese, shredded
salt and freshly ground black pepper
1 tablespoon chopped fresh parsley, for garnish

FILLING:

1 tablespoon corn oil
1 large onion, coarsely chopped
1 large eggplant, cut into
1-inch cubes
3 small zucchini, sliced
1 sweet green pepper, cored, seeded
and chopped
1 red pepper, cored, seeded and chopped
10 ounces tomatoes, peeled, quartered
and seeded
2 tablespoons tomato paste
1 teaspoon sugar
1 tablespoon chopped fresh basil, or 1 teaspoon
dried basil

To make the choux pastry or gougère, put the butter or margarine, the measured water and ¼ teaspoon of salt in a large saucepan. Have the flour ready nearby. Bring the butter and water mixture to a fast boil, remove the pan from the heat and tip in the flour all at once. Beat briskly with a wooden spoon until the mixture forms a ball that rolls cleanly around the pan. Let cool for about 5 minutes.

Slowly add the beaten eggs, a little at a time, beating well between each addition. (An electric whisk makes this job quick and easy.) When all the egg is incorporated, beat in plenty of black pepper, the mustard and the shredded cheese.

Place adjoining heaped teaspoons of the mixture in a 10-inch circle on a greased baking sheet, leaving rough peaks. Bake in a preheated oven, 425°F, for about 40 minutes or until the choux pastry is puffy and brown.

Meanwhile, make the filling. Heat the oil in a saucepan and cook the onion gently without browning for about 10 minutes. Add the eggplant, zucchini, peppers and tomatoes. Stir in the tomato paste, sugar and basil, and season with salt and pepper. Cover the pan and simmer gently for a further 15 minutes, stirring once or twice during cooking.

Transfer the hot choux ring to a warmed serving plate and spoon in the ratatouille filling. Serve immediately, sprinkled with chopped fresh parsley, accompanied by a crisp green salad.

SHRIMP & CHILI QUICHE

Serves 6
½ cup all-purpose flour, plus extra for dusting
pinch of salt
½ stick butter or margarine
1 tablespoon cold water
sprigs of fresh parsley, for garnish

FILLING:
2 eggs
¾ cup light cream
2 tablespoons all-purpose flour
¾ teaspoon garlic salt
2 ounces Cheddar cheese, shredded
2 ounces Gruyère cheese, shredded
1 small onion, finely chopped
2 fresh green chiles, seeded and chopped
⅓ cup cooked peeled shrimp

To make the dough, sift the flour and salt into a bowl. Add the butter or margarine and rub in using your fingertips until the mixture resembles fine bread crumbs. Add the water and mix in with a knife, then knead lightly until the mixture forms a dough. Form into a smooth ball and let rest in the refrigerator for about 30 minutes.

Turn the dough out onto a lightly floured surface, roll out and use to line a 8-inch pie pan or ring. To bake, prick the bottom of the dough with a fork and fill the pastry case with a circle of waxed paper topped with baking beans. Place on a baking sheet and cook in a preheated oven, 450°F, for 6-10 minutes, until the dough is lightly browned. Remove the dough case from the oven and reduce the oven temperature to 350°F. Remove the waxed paper and beans.

For the filling, beat together the eggs, light cream, flour and garlic salt (the mixture need not be smooth). Stir in the shredded cheeses, onion and green chiles.

Pour the filling into the dough case and sprinkle the shrimp on top of the filling. Cook the quiche in the preheated oven for about 35-40 minutes, or until a knife inserted in the center comes out clean.

Let cool for about 15 minutes before serving, garnished with sprigs of parsley.

STIR-FRIED SQUID & PEPPERS

Serves 4

1-1¼ pounds squid
2 tablespoons corn oil
1 teaspoon sesame oil
1 sweet red pepper, cored, seeded and cut
into strips
1 sweet green pepper, cored, seeded and cut
into strips
1 small bunch of scallions, shredded
3 celery stalks, sliced
little lemon juice
salt and freshly ground black pepper

FOR GARNISH:
flat-leaf parsley
lemon wedges

First, wash the squid. Pull the head and tentacles away from the body, then pull the cartilage or quill out of the body pouch and discard it. Cut off the head and mouth at the base of the tentacles and discard them. Wash the body and the tentacles, peeling off any dark skin. Chop the tentacles and cut the body into rings.

Heat the oils in a wok or skillet, add the peppers, scallions and celery and stir-fry for 3 minutes. Add the squid and stir-fry for 3-4 minutes. Do not cook any longer, as this will toughen the squid. Add seasoning and lemon juice. Serve with parsley and lemon wedges.

SMOKY CHILIED SHRIMP

Serves 4

10 green chiles, seeded and halved lengthwise
20 raw king-size shrimp, peeled, with tails
left intact
5 tablespoons olive oil
salt
lemon wedges, to serve

Wrap one half of each chili around the middle of each shrimp and thread 5 shrimp onto each of 4 metal or soaked bamboo skewers.

Place the skewers in a long shallow dish and sprinkle over the oil and the salt. Cover the dish and let marinate in a cool place for about 30 minutes.

Cook the shrimp on the oiled grill of a preheated barbecue, or under a preheated broiler, for 3 minutes on each side, basting with any remaining marinade. Serve the shrimp hot with lemon wedges.

Illustrated opposite

TUNA STEAKS WITH GREEN PEPPERS

Serves 4-6

**2 pounds fresh tuna steaks, cut ¾-inch thick and
dusted with seasoned all-purpose flour
6 tablespoons olive oil
2 sweet green peppers
2 onions, sliced
2 large tomatoes, quartered
1 garlic clove, crushed
1 bouquet garni
¾ cup dry white wine
salt and freshly ground black pepper**

Gently sauté the floured tuna steaks in half of the olive oil in a large skillet. Place in an ovenproof dish.

Meanwhile, place the peppers under a hot broiler until the skins blister and blacken, then carefully peel off the skins. Core, seed and slice the peppers.

Cook the onions in the rest of the oil until tender. Add the peppers, tomatoes, garlic and bouquet garni. Season to taste. Simmer for 20 minutes. Add the wine and return to a boil.

Cover the tuna steaks with the sauce. Bake in a preheated oven, 400°F, for 20 minutes, reduce the oven temperature to 325°F, cover, and cook for a further 30 minutes.

HADDOCK IN CHILI SAUCE

Serves 4

**4 tablespoons corn oil
2 large onions, sliced
3 garlic cloves, crushed
1½ pounds haddock fillets, cut into chunks
2 tablespoons all-purpose flour
1 teaspoon turmeric
4 fresh green chiles, seeded and chopped
2 tablespoons lemon juice
¾ cup thick coconut milk
salt
chili flowers, to garnish (*optional – see below*)**

Heat the oil in a skillet, add the onions and cook until soft and golden. Add the garlic and cook for 30 seconds. Remove from the skillet with a slotted spoon and set aside.

Toss the fish in the flour, add to the skillet, stir in the turmeric and chiles and cook for 1 minute. Stir in the lemon juice, coconut milk and salt to taste, then simmer, uncovered, for 10 minutes, stirring until the sauce thickens. Return the onion mixture to the skillet and heat for 2-3 minutes. Spoon into a warmed dish and garnish with chili flowers, if using.

Note: To make the chili flowers, shred the chiles lengthwise, leaving ½-inch attached at the stem end. Place them in ice water for about 1 hour to open.

ITALIAN HERBY MUSSELS

Serves 4

4 pounds fresh mussels
2 tablespoons butter
2 tablespoons oil
4 celery stalks, sliced
1 sweet red pepper, cored, seeded and chopped
1 sweet yellow pepper, cored, seeded and chopped
2 garlic cloves, crushed
2-inch strip of lemon rind
1 bay leaf
6 tablespoons dry white wine
½ cup fresh white bread crumbs
4 eggs, beaten
2 tablespoons light cream
¼ teaspoon turmeric
2 tablespoons shredded Parmesan cheese
salt and freshly ground black pepper

To prepare the mussels, discard any broken shells and any that are open and remain so even when tapped lightly. Wash the mussels several times in cold water and place in a large bowl. Scrub the shells to remove any dirt or barnacles. Pull off the "beards" that protrude from the hinges and wash again.

Heat the butter and oil in a large shallow ovenproof casserole dish. Add the celery and peppers and then cook until softened. Add the garlic, lemon rind, bay leaf, mussels and wine. Season with salt and pepper.

Cover and cook over a high heat for 2-3 minutes, shaking constantly. Remove any opened mussels and set aside, then cover and cook for 1 minute more. Discard any mussels that have not opened. Drain and reserve the liquid from the casserole dish.

Pull off and discard the empty top shell from each mussel. Return the mussels to the casserole dish, and sprinkle with the bread crumbs.

Beat together the eggs, cream, turmeric and 6 tablespoons of the reserved cooking liquid, and season with salt and pepper. Pour over the mussels and sprinkle the cheese on top. Cook in a preheated oven, 400°F, for 10-15 minutes, until set and golden. Serve hot with French bread.

CHILI CHICKEN
WITH PINE NUTS

Serves 4

4 boneless, skinless chicken breasts, about
¼ to ½ pound each
4 tablespoons corn oil
1 sweet red pepper, cored, seeded and cut into
thin strips
1 sweet green pepper, cored, seeded and cut
into thin strips
1 fresh red chili, seeded and finely chopped
1 fresh green chili, seeded and finely chopped
¼ cup pine nuts
1 garlic clove, finely chopped
4 tablespoons dry white wine
2 tablespoons lemon juice
3 tablespoons oyster sauce
2 teaspoons sugar
1 teaspoon chili sauce
4 tablespoons light soy sauce
1 tablespoon cornstarch
salt and freshly ground black pepper
2 scallions, sliced diagonally, for garnish

Pat the chicken breasts dry with paper towels, then cut each chicken piece into ½ x 2-inch strips. Sprinkle with salt and pepper. Pour 2 tablespoons of the oil into a wok or large skillet, place over a high heat and add the chicken strips. Cook, stirring constantly, for 5 minutes, or until tender. Remove the chicken and reserve.

Heat the remaining oil in the wok or skillet and stir-fry the red and green pepper strips for 2 minutes, until just cooked. Lift out and reserve.

Cook the chiles, pine nuts and garlic over a medium heat for 1 minute. Drain off and discard any excess fat, then add the white wine, lemon juice, oyster sauce, sugar and chili sauce. Cook, stirring frequently, for 1 minute.

Blend the soy sauce and cornstarch together, then add to the chili mixture and bring to a boil. Return the cooked chicken and pepper strips to the wok or skillet, then cover and cook over a medium heat until the chicken has warmed through.

To serve, place the chicken mixture on a warmed serving plate, and sprinkle with the sliced scallions.

Illustrated opposite

RED PEPPER CHICKEN

Serves 4

2 tablespoons butter
3 tablespoons corn oil
4 boneless, skinless chicken breasts
1 onion, finely chopped
2 garlic cloves, finely chopped
2 sweet red peppers, cored, seeded and thinly sliced
1 pound tomatoes, peeled and sliced
1 tablespoon tomato paste
2 teaspoons red wine vinegar
4 tablespoons stuffed green olives, sliced
1 teaspoon soft dark brown sugar
pinch of ground cumin
2 tablespoons chopped fresh parsley
salt and freshly ground black pepper

Heat the butter and 2 tablespoons of oil in a skillet and cook the chicken 5 minutes on each side. Remove from the skillet and keep warm.

Add the remaining oil to the skillet and sauté the onion and garlic for 3 minutes, stirring occasionally. Add the peppers and cook for about 2 minutes. Then add the tomatoes, tomato paste, vinegar, olives, sugar, cumin and seasoning. Bring to a boil and simmer, uncovered, for 15 minutes. Return the chicken to the skillet and simmer for 15 minutes, or until the chicken is cooked. Stir in the parsley and adjust the seasoning to taste.

CHINESE CHICKEN

Serves 4

½ pound boneless, skinless chicken, cut into thin strips
½ teaspoon salt
1 tablespoon soy sauce
1 egg white
1 tablespoon cornstarch
5 tablespoons corn oil
2 slices of fresh ginger, shredded
2-3 shallots, cut into thin strips
1 fresh hot chili, cut into thin strips
1 sweet green and 1 red pepper, cored, seeded and cut into thin strips
2-3 celery stalks, cut into thin strips
2 tablespoons black bean sauce

Put the chicken in a bowl with the salt, soy sauce, egg white and cornstarch, and mix well. Heat the oil in a wok or skillet, add the chicken and stir-fry over a moderate heat for 2-3 minutes. Remove from the skillet.

Increase the heat to high. When the oil starts to smoke, put the ginger in the skillet with the shallots, chili, peppers and celery. Stir well, then add the black bean sauce and continue cooking for a few seconds.

Return the chicken to the skillet and stir-fry for 1-1½ minutes, or until the meat is tender, but the vegetables are still crisp and crunchy. Serve immediately.

CHICKEN & PEPPER CURRY

Serves 4

**2 large sweet red peppers, or 1 sweet yellow
and 1 sweet red pepper, cored, seeded
and chopped**
1 large onion, chopped
3 garlic cloves, chopped
1-inch piece of fresh ginger, peeled and chopped
2 tablespoons unsweetened dehydrated coconut
2 tablespoons lime or lemon juice
1 cup water
2 tablespoons corn oil
1 tablespoon garam masala (*see note below*)
1 teaspoon hot curry powder
¼ teaspoon chili powder
**2 pounds small boneless, skinless
chicken pieces**
4 tablespoons thick yogurt
salt and freshly ground black pepper

FOR GARNISH:
paprika
sprigs of fresh parsley

Place the peppers in a blender or food processor with the onion, garlic, ginger, coconut and lime or lemon juice. Add 3 tablespoons of the measured water and work to a smooth paste.

Heat the oil in a large ovenproof casserole dish or saucepan over a moderate heat. Add the garam masala and curry powder and stir-fry for a few seconds. Add the prepared vegetable paste, the chili powder and salt and pepper to taste. Stir the mixture well and bring slowly to a boil.

Add the chicken pieces to the casserole dish with the remaining water and mix thoroughly. Return to a boil, then lower the heat, cover and simmer for about 35 minutes, stirring several times. Stir in 3 tablespoons of the yogurt, cover and cook for a further 5 minutes, stirring frequently.

Transfer to a warmed serving dish, spoon over the remaining yogurt and sprinkle with paprika. Garnish with sprigs of parsley and serve with basmati rice and chili pickle.

Note: If you cannot buy garam masala, you can make your own by grinding together ½ teaspoon green cardamom seeds, ¼ teaspoon cumin seeds and ¼ teaspoon cloves.

MICROWAVE METHOD: Place the peppers, onion, garlic, ginger, coconut and lime or lemon juice in a blender or food processor. Add 3 tablespoons water and blend to a smooth paste. Place the oil, garam masala and curry powder in a casserole dish and cook on High for 30 seconds. Add the vegetable paste, chili powder and seasoning and cook on High for 2 minutes. Add chicken and remaining water, cover and cook on High for 10 minutes. Stir. Reduce to Medium and cook for 15 minutes. Stir in the yogurt, sprinkle with paprika and garnish as above.

THAI PORK CURRY

Serves 4

4 tablespoons clarified butter
2-8 garlic cloves, according to taste,
finely chopped
1 onion, sliced
1 tablespoon mild curry paste
1 cup water
1-inch piece of fresh ginger, peeled and
thinly sliced
1-6 fresh red chiles, according to taste, sliced
2 tablespoons Thai fish sauce (*nam pla*) or
puréed anchovy fillets
1½ pounds pork fillet, cut into large cubes
1 sweet red pepper, puréed
6-8 dried or fresh lime leaves (*optional*)
2 tablespoons thick, unsweetened coconut milk
1 tablespoon chopped fresh cilantro leaves
2 teaspoons chopped fresh basil leaves
salt
sprigs of fresh cilantro leaves, for garnish

Heat the clarified butter in a large skillet or wok and stir-fry the garlic for about 1 minute. Add the sliced onion and stir-fry until it is soft and translucent.

Add the curry paste and the measured water, stirring until blended – Thai curries are fairly runny. Add the ginger, chiles and the fish sauce or anchovy fillets and simmer for about 3-4 minutes. Transfer this mixture to a heavy casserole dish and stir in the pork.

Cover the casserole dish with a lid, then place in a preheated oven, 375°F, and bake for 20 minutes. Add the remaining ingredients, with a little water to moisten if necessary, and return to the oven to cook for a further 40 minutes.

Just before serving, season with salt to taste and spoon off any excess oil. Garnish with sprigs of cilantro and serve at once, with plain boiled rice.

MICROWAVE METHOD: Place the butter, garlic and onion in a casserole dish. Cook on High for 2 minutes. Add the curry paste, 1 cup hot water, the ginger, chiles and anchovy fillets and cook on High for 3 minutes. Stir in the pork. Cook on High for 5 minutes. Add the remaining ingredients. Cook on High for 5 minutes, then reduce power to Medium for 15 minutes and serve as above.

Illustrated opposite

INDONESIAN STEAK WITH CHILI

Serves 4

1½ pounds rump steak
2 teaspoons ground coriander
2 tablespoons tamarind water or lime juice
1 teaspoon brown sugar
8 fresh red chiles, seeded and chopped
4 shallots or 1 onion, chopped
2 garlic cloves, chopped
6 tablespoons corn oil
1 teaspoon lemon juice
salt and freshly ground black pepper

Using a sharp knife, slice the meat thinly across the grain, then cut the slices into 2-inch squares. Arrange in a single layer on a large plate and sprinkle with the coriander, tamarind water or lime juice, sugar and salt and pepper. Press each piece of meat with your hands so that the spices and flavorings are thoroughly absorbed into the meat, then spread the slices out on the plate again. Cover with plastic wrap and then let stand for 2-3 hours in a cool place.

Put the chopped chiles, shallots or onion and garlic in a blender or food processor and work until they are just broken down, but not reduced to a paste.

Heat the oil in a large heavy skillet. Add the squares of seasoned meat and cook, stirring frequently, until evenly browned and cooked through. Remove from the skillet with a slotted spoon and keep hot.

Add the pounded chili mixture to the oil remaining in the skillet and cook for 2-3 minutes, stirring constantly.

Return the meat to the skillet and stir well, until coated with the chili mixture. Add the lemon juice and salt to taste and stir well. Serve the steak hot with plain boiled rice and a selection of relishes and pickles.

BEEF PEPPERPOT

Serves 4

2 tablespoons all-purpose flour
1½ pounds braising steak, trimmed and cut into
2 x 1-inch strips
2 tablespoons butter
2 tablespoons corn oil
1 large Spanish onion, thinly sliced
1 garlic clove, crushed
2 cans (*about 14 ounces each*) tomatoes
2 teaspoons black peppercorns, lightly crushed
2 teaspoons paprika
1 sweet red pepper, cored, seeded and sliced
1 large sweet green pepper, cored, seeded
and sliced
salt and freshly ground black pepper

TO SERVE:
4-6 tablespoons sour cream
1 teaspoon paprika

Season the flour with salt and toss the strips of meat in the seasoned flour. Heat the butter and 1 tablespoon of the oil in a large skillet and cook the floured meat, turning until it is browned all over. Remove the meat from the skillet with a slotted spoon and transfer to a casserole dish.

Cook the onion and garlic in the same skillet until lightly browned, adding the remaining oil if necessary. Add any remaining seasoned flour and cook, stirring, for 1 minute.

Remove the skillet from the heat and stir in the tomatoes and their juice, the crushed black peppercorns and the paprika. Return to the heat, bring to a boil and simmer for about 1 minute, stirring.

Pour the tomato mixture over the meat in the casserole dish, then cover tightly. Cook in a preheated oven, 325°F, for 1½ hours, then stir in the sliced peppers. Cover and continue cooking for a further 1 hour, or until the meat is tender.

Adjust the seasoning to taste. Spoon the sour cream into the casserole dish, then sprinkle with paprika and freshly ground black pepper and serve hot.

MICROWAVE METHOD: Place the butter and oil in a large casserole dish and cook on High for 30-40 seconds. Toss the meat in seasoned flour. Add to the casserole dish and cook on High for 5 minutes, stirring twice. Add the onion and garlic and cook on High for 3 minutes. Add the tomatoes, peppercorns and paprika. Cover the casserole dish and cook on High for 10 minutes. Reduce power to Low for 1 hour. Add the peppers and cook on Medium-Low for 40 minutes.

BEEF & PORK CHILI

Serves 8
2 slices of lean bacon, chopped
1 pound braising steak, cut into
½-inch cubes
1 pound lean shoulder or hand of pork, cut into
½-inch cubes
2 onions, sliced
2 garlic cloves, crushed
½ teaspoon dried oregano
½ teaspoon ground cumin
½ teaspoon ground coriander
2 fresh green chiles, seeded and chopped
¾ cup beef stock
¾ cup red wine
1 can (*about 14 ounces*) tomatoes
1 sweet green pepper, cored, seeded and sliced
½ cup strained tomatoes
salt

Place the chopped bacon in a large saucepan and cook until fairly crisp. Add the steak, pork, onions and garlic and cook until the meat is brown. Stir in the oregano, cumin, coriander, chiles, stock, wine, tomatoes and their juice, green pepper, strained tomatoes and 1 teaspoon of salt.

Cover and simmer for 1½ hours, or until the meat is tender, stirring occasionally. Serve hot with plain boiled rice and a green salad.

STIR-FRIED BEEF WITH PEPPERS

Serves 4
1 tablespoon olive oil
1 red onion, sliced
1 large garlic clove, cut into slivers
1 pound fillet steak, cut into thin strips
2 sweet yellow peppers, cored, seeded and cut into strips
1 fresh green chili, seeded and chopped
1 tablespoon soy sauce
2 tablespoons dry sherry
1 tablespoon tiny sprigs of fresh rosemary
salt and freshly ground black pepper

Heat the olive oil in a wok or deep skillet and stir-fry the sliced onion and garlic for 2 minutes. Add the strips of beef and stir-fry briskly until evenly browned on all sides and almost tender.

Add the strips of pepper and the chili and stir-fry for a further 2 minutes. Add the soy sauce, sherry, rosemary and salt and pepper to taste and stir-fry for a further 1-2 minutes. Serve hot with plain boiled rice.

Illustrated opposite

LAMB & PEPPER CASSEROLE

Serves 4

2 pounds neck of lamb cutlets
all-purpose flour, for coating
2 tablespoons olive oil
2 garlic cloves, crushed
1 cup dry white wine
3 sweet red peppers, cored, seeded
and quartered
3 sweet green peppers, cored, seeded
and quartered
3 tomatoes, peeled and quartered
1 bay leaf
salt and freshly ground black pepper

Trim any excess fat from the lamb, season with salt and pepper, and coat with flour.

Heat the olive oil in a large ovenproof casserole dish, and sauté the garlic for about 1 minute. Add the lamb and sauté until lightly browned, turning once or twice. Pour in the wine and allow to bubble briskly for a few minutes, or until reduced by one-third.

Add the peppers, tomatoes and bay leaf to the lamb. Cover tightly and simmer very gently for 45 minutes, or until the lamb is tender. Remove and discard the bay leaf. Adjust the seasoning to taste and serve the lamb immediately from the casserole dish, accompanied by rice or noodles.

HUNGARIAN PEPPERS WITH CHICKEN & VEAL

Serves 4

2 tablespoons oil
¾ pounds veal, chopped
1 pound boneless, skinless chicken
breast, chopped
3-4 sweet green peppers, cored, seeded
and chopped
2 onions, chopped
1 cup chicken stock
a little paprika
½ cup sour cream
salt and freshly ground black pepper
chopped fresh parsley, for garnish

Heat the oil in an ovenproof casserole dish. Add the veal and chicken and cook, stirring, over a high heat until lightly browned.

Add the chopped peppers and onions and cook for 2-3 minutes. Pour in the stock and season with salt, pepper and paprika to taste. Cover the casserole dish and simmer over a low heat for about 40 minutes, or until the meat is tender, stirring occasionally.

Stir in the sour cream and serve immediately, garnished with chopped parsley, accompanied by plain boiled rice or baby potatoes and sautéed zucchini.

KEEMA PIMENTO

Serves 4-6

1 sweet green pepper, cored, seeded and cut
into strips

3 tablespoons corn oil

2 onions, chopped

½ teaspoon ground cumin

2 teaspoons garam masala (*see page 51*)

¼ teaspoon ground cinnamon

1 teaspoon chili powder

1½ pounds chopped beef or lamb

beef stock or water (*optional*)

salt and freshly ground black pepper

slices of sweet green pepper, for garnish

Cook the strips of pepper in the oil for about 1 minute, then remove from the pan with a slotted spoon and set aside. Cook the onions in the oil remaining in the pan until golden brown. Mix 1 teaspoon each of salt and pepper with the spices and add to the onions. Cook for 2 minutes, stirring continuously.

Add the chopped meat and cook over a low heat, stirring occasionally to make sure it does not stick to the pan. Add a little beef stock or water, if necessary. Cook for about 20 minutes, then add the reserved green pepper and continue cooking for 10 minutes.

Garnish with slices of green pepper. Serve with rice and a selection of accompaniments such as peach or mango chutney.

JAMBALAYA

Serves 4

½ stick butter

2 garlic cloves, crushed

1 pound ham, cut into bite-size cubes

1 pound boneless, skinless chicken breast, cut
into bite-size cubes

1 large onion, chopped

1 sweet green and 1 sweet red pepper, cored,
seeded and chopped

4 fresh green chiles, seeded and thinly sliced

1 cup long-grain rice

½ teaspoon turmeric

2 cups chicken stock

dash of Tabasco sauce

1 cup cooked peeled shrimp

salt and freshly ground black pepper

paprika, for sprinkling

Melt the butter in a large skillet and add the garlic, ham, chicken and salt and pepper; cook until the chicken is browned. Add the onion, peppers and chiles and continue cooking until the onion has softened slightly. Stir in the rice and turmeric, reduce the heat, then pour in the stock and add the Tabasco. Stir well and bring to a boil, cover and reduce the heat so that the jambalaya simmers gently. Cook for 10 minutes before adding the shrimp, then cook for a further 5-10 minutes, or until the rice is cooked and most of the stock has been absorbed to leave a moist dish. Sprinkle with a little paprika before serving.

PEPPER RELISH

Makes about 4 pounds

6 sweet red peppers, cored and seeded
6 sweet green peppers, cored and seeded
6 onions
3 garlic cloves, crushed
1 cup vinegar
¾ cup soft brown sugar
1 tablespoon celery seeds
dash of Tabasco sauce
1 tablespoon salt

Shred both the peppers and onions using the shredding disc of a food processor. Alternatively, chop the vegetables finely.

Put all the shredded vegetables into a strainer and pour boiling water over them. Drain, then place in a heavy-bottom saucepan with all the remaining ingredients and bring to a boil, stirring occasionally. Reduce the heat and simmer for 30 minutes.

Meanwhile, sterilize and have ready warmed, dry jars. Pour the relish into the jars, seal and label. Serve the relish with hot or cold meats, sausages or cheese. The relish may be kept for up to 6-8 weeks in the refrigerator.

RED PEPPER & ZUCCHINI PICKLE

Makes 2-3 pounds

3 sweet red peppers, cored, seeded and coarsely chopped
10 ounces zucchini, coarsely chopped
10 ounces cooking apples, peeled, cored and chopped
12 ounces onions, chopped
¼ cup raisins
¼ cup golden raisins
1 cup brown sugar
1 teaspoon ground ginger
½ teaspoon turmeric
1 cup vinegar
salt

Place the peppers and zucchini in a bowl. Sprinkle with salt, cover and let stand for several hours or overnight. Drain, rinse well and dry. Place the apples and onions in a pan. Add the peppers, zucchini and remaining ingredients. Bring to a boil, cover and simmer for 15 minutes. Uncover the pan and cook for a further 1 hour.

Meanwhile, sterilize and have ready warmed, dry jars. Bottle, seal and label. The pickle may be kept for up to 6-8 weeks.

Illustrated opposite